LEADERS' MAP

Helping doers think and thinkers do™

John D.H. Greenway

Published in 2013 by John D. H. Greenway

Copyright © 2013 John D. H. Greenway.

John D. H. Greenway has asserted his right under the Copyright, Designs and Patents Act 1988 to be identified as the author of this work.

All rights reserved. No part of this publication may be reproduced, stored in a retrieval system, or transmitted in any form or by any means, electronic, mechanical, photocopying, recording or otherwise, without the prior permission of the copyright owner.

Contents

Section A	**Setting the Scene**	**1**
Chapter 1	Purpose	3
Chapter 2	Non-Negotiables	7
Chapter 3	Your Roles	17
Section B	**Mapping Concepts**	**25**
Chapter 4	Mapping Your Journey	27
Chapter 5	Navigating Your Way Through	33
Section C	**Navigation Principles**	**39**
Chapter 6	See the Big Picture	41
Chapter 7	Choose the Right Direction	49
Chapter 8	Do the Right Things	57
Chapter 9	Check Progress	71
Chapter 10	Be Inspired	77
Section D	**Applications**	**85**
Chapter 11	Becoming an All-Weather Leader	87
Chapter 12	Takeaways	95
Chapter 13	New Steps	101
Appendix	**Leaders' Map App**	**105**

Section A

Setting the Scene

- 1. Purpose
- 2. Non-negotiables
- 3. Your roles

A. Setting the Scene

- 4. Mapping your journey
- 5. Navigating your way through

B. Mapping Concept

Leaders' Map: navigating towards success

- 6. See the Big Picture
- 7. Choose the Right Direction
- 8. Do the Right Things
- 9. Check Progress
- 10. Be Inspired

C. Navigation Principles

- 11. Becoming an All-Weather Leader
- 12. Takeaways
- 13. New steps

D. Applications

CHAPTER 1

PURPOSE

"Previous journeys in search of treasure have taught me that a zigzag strategy is the best way to get ahead."
Tahir Shah

"The real voyage of discovery consists not in seeking new lands, but seeing with new eyes."
Marcel Proust

This book is written to enable and empower you.

It is written to help you navigate towards success in your work… and other roles in your life. It's about your journeys.

You are probably already in some leadership role, or certainly aspiring to be. You may be an entrepreneur or a business leader or managing a team for the first time. You may have leading responsibilities in the public sector, a social enterprise, a sports club or a community group. You may even just be running the most important organisation of all – your family.

In fact, you are likely to have a variety of leadership roles in your life, and all of them are very important to you.

The common denominator is a desire to move forward in a purposeful direction and take people with you. You want to get "somewhere" and you are prepared to take the lead.

Your Challenge

Most plans, whether they are in business or in your personal life, go something like this: "We are here and we want to get there".

There is a gap between your current and future location. A straight line is then drawn to bridge the gap.

It seems so simple, but life does not often work out like that, at least not in my experience.

Chapter 1: Purpose

Life is unpredictable and circumstances change. Winds blow, waves rise and currents pull. Unseen obstacles block your way and unexpected opportunities present themselves. Instead of clarity, confusion can arise. The future can suddenly be shrouded in a mist. Progress can be side-tracked or grind to a halt.

Your journey is often much more like sailing the seas than driving along a straight road.

There are no signposts to tell you to turn right or left, you have to use your judgement to tack or pivot, otherwise you can blissfully go way off course while you think you are sailing well.

Your Map

To get where you have been before may not require a map, but to get where you have never been before certainly will.

Leaders' Map is not a road map which you just have to follow, but a map that you will have to create - because your journey is unique. It is a framework that is applicable and adaptable to any leadership role. But you will need to do the mapping.

This book is written to enable you to:

- Map your journey/s
- Navigate your way to success in your various roles
- Become an "All-Weather Leader"

So what's to come?

We will be covering a range of topics:

- Understanding something about the captain of the boat – you
- The journeys that you have to make – your work and other roles in your life
- How to do your mapping – the Leaders' Map concept
- How to navigate successfully – the 5 principles of Leaders' Map
- How to develop into an All-Weather Leader – the aim of Leaders' Map

The book is a distillation of thinking and experience that has come from working with leaders in global corporates, fledgling businesses, social enterprises and community-based organisations. It is based on things that have worked and informed by things that have failed. It's derived from working with individuals and teams. All case examples are bona-fide, with names changed to protect the innocent!

If in some small way it helps you to navigate more successfully, then my job is done.

Enjoy the journey!

CHAPTER 2

NON-NEGOTIABLES

"Thinkers think and doers do. But until the thinkers do and the doers think, progress will be just another word."
François de La Rochefoucauld

"Don't judge each day by the harvest you reap, but by the seeds that you plant."
Robert Louis Stevenson

The USS Montana was somewhere in the Irish Sea.

The sea was rough and visibility was very poor. A tense conversation took place between the American Captain of the USS Montana and an Irish radio operator.

> American: *Again this is the USS Montana requesting that you IMMEDIATELY divert your course 15 degrees to the north to avoid a collision…. Over.*
>
> Irishman: *Please divert YOUR course 15 degrees to the south to avoid collision…. Over.*
>
> American: *This is Captain Hancock. You WILL divert your course!…. Over.*
>
> Irishman: *Negative, Captain. I'm NOT moving anything. Change your course….. Over.*
>
> American: *So, this is the USS Montana, the second largest vessel in the North Atlantic Fleet. You will change course 15 degrees north or I will be forced to take measures to ensure the safety of this ship….. OVER!!*
>
> Irishman: *This is a lighthouse! It's YOUR call.*

The old stories are the best. Different versions of this story go back a long way. This version was the script from an award winning Swedish TV advertisement.

The relevance of this story for us is that there are some things in life that, by their very nature, will not change. They are non-negotiable. They are fixed. However much the Captain issued threats, the lighthouse was not going to move, so he had either to adjust his course or suffer the consequences.

Chapter 2: Non-Negotiables

I want to highlight two non-negotiables that you will have to work with on your voyage. The better you understand them, the better the progress you will make on your journey. The first is your personality and the second is a principle of life.

1. Know thyself.

This is an ancient Greek aphorism from the temple at Delphi. If you know your own strengths and weaknesses you will be in a much stronger position to maximise your potential and manage your limitations.

I have spent a significant part of my career helping leaders and organisations to understand the impact of personality upon performance, behaviour and results. One thing that I have learned is that although you may be able to change your behaviour, your personality is much more fixed. It is the nature of things.

You can't train a dog to climb a tree. It will be incredibly frustrating for both owner and dog, and I am sure that the tree will not be too pleased either. Time would be better spent chasing sticks, rounding up sheep, barking and doing other useful dog activities.

One question about your personality that is important to explore and understand is:

Are you a Doer or a Thinker?

We are all a blend of the two. We all have a Dan Doer and Tom Thinker, but most of us will have a clear tendency towards one more than the other. What is your percentage split – 90/10 … 20/80…65/35? Be honest with yourself and don't just give yourself a "wish score". What would a colleague or friend say?

It is self-evident that your "thinking/doing combination" will affect the way you see and respond to things. Although it may be your natural starting point it doesn't have to be the finishing line. You can choose to do something about it.

How does your "thinking/doing combination" currently impact on the way you:

- Set direction
- Make decisions
- Work with other people
- Get things done

Don't try to change your personality, but rather focus your efforts on changing your behaviours to become more effective. Your effort should not be spent on trying to change the nature of things, but on how to nurture the nature.

But how can you get Dan Doer and Tom Thinker working better together? Often they seem to work independently. Dan Doer is focused on action today and dealing with tangibles. Tom Thinker is much more comfortable with ideas for tomorrow and kicking around concepts. Well, they need to have a meeting-place, a place where they will talk and work together.

Chapter 2: Non-Negotiables

Let me give an example. I have often seen in organisations that the strategic guys, who are focused on the Macro, and the operational guys, who are focused on the Micro, don't communicate well. They often don't naturally understand one another or appreciate their differing challenges and priorities. They are coming at things from very different angles. They need to meet, talk, discuss and kick things around together. They need a meeting-place that they can both get to.

This mid-tier is the Meso level. Most operational Dan Doers in an organisation can stretch up to the Meso area, even if they can't make it to the Macro level. Most strategic Tom Thinkers can stretch down to the Meso level, even if they can't make it to the Micro. If they work together in the Meso Meeting Place some of the time and get to understand each other they will become all the more effective as an organisation. It requires team work.

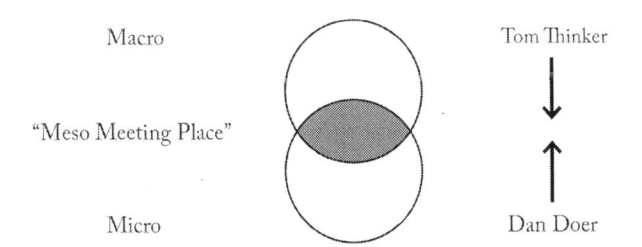

Macro

"Meso Meeting Place"

Micro

Tom Thinker
↓
↑
Dan Doer

In the same way, we also need to connect our doing and thinking in our own Meso Meeting Place. As it may not happen naturally, you will have to be intentional about it, just like getting the strategic and operational guys together in a meeting.

How might this work for you?

For example, if you are a Dan Doer diarise some thinking time and turn off your phone. Jot down your questions, thoughts and ideas. Widen and lengthen your horizons and complete the following sentences "In 3 years' time…" and "Next year…" and "In a month's time…"

As big questions come to the forefront of your mind, kick them around with your team. Hold back on giving your solutions… and listen.

If you are a Tom Thinker you will instinctively go through much of this thought process. Your challenge is to focus and engage well with your stakeholders. Why not share the bigger picture with your customers and ask "So what needs to be done in the next x weeks to move us forward?"

In other words, do something that you wouldn't normally do. Break the routine. Be accountable to others. Show some imagination and make it fun! And keep doing it.

So, we have been thinking about our natural personality, but what is the natural life principle that will help us on our voyage?

2. The principle of Ut Severis Seges.

Did you have a school motto?

I did. It was three Latin words, *Ut Severis Seges.*

Chapter 2: Non-Negotiables

It means "As you sow, so shall you reap". It is a quotation taken from the book of Galatians in the Bible. What does it mean? In its simplest form it means if you sow a yam, you will get a yam, and not wheat. If you sow a melon you will harvest a melon, and not an orange. You harvest what you sow. You get out what you put in.

Let's apply the principle to a work setting. If you are in sales with an exclusive license for a new drilling product for gas exploration, but you don't make any customer calls, don't be surprised that nobody buys the product. It is a simple case of inputs and outputs.

If we take it a step beyond a yam, melon or brand new drilling product we see that it is a variation on the law of cause and effect.

Zig Ziglar, the American author and speaker, said "Every choice you make has a result". There is a consequence. It is the natural order of things. You can trace things back from the result to the actions to the choice. If you had made a different choice or taken different actions you would have a different result.

Sow seeds in the right soil, at the right time of year, with the right weather conditions and you will get a crop. Sow seeds in the wrong place, at the wrong time in the wrong conditions and you will have to buy your bread from the bakery.

We all see this principle operating positively or negatively on a daily basis. For example, I recall the case of a particular energy services business. Pre-2008, it was under-performing simply because they seemed more interested in the seed bag itself, rather than scattering the seeds. They were more interested in making things perfect internally rather than concerning themselves about their customers' headaches. However, following a change of leadership they eventually recognised that their poor results were a consequence of their own actions and during the toughest trading period in living memory set about systematically and purposefully scattering the seed in the right places. They started to focus on their customers' issues and became intentional in how they could offer fresh solutions. Five years later they are reaping the benefits with a billion pound order book and are sector leading. A true transformation.

It is perhaps even more evident in smaller, entrepreneurial organisations where decisions and actions have a quicker and bigger impact, either positively or negatively.

I think of five young entrepreneurs in diverse sectors – social media, fashion, construction, recruitment and product design – who have applied the *Ut Severis Seges* principle. Through the same precarious trading period they have survived and thrived. Each one of them has had to wrestle with very different problems, but they understood how to sow in the right way for their specific business. One stopped doing reactive one-off projects and focused on long-term customers, another invested much more time in developing their people, another increased their physical sales presence, another "sowed their seeds" into customer service and the final one focused their personal effort on improving their PR to attract investment. They are now reaping…but they continue to sow.

In summary, we have been talking about two non-negotiables - things that you can't change, but that you can understand and use to your advantage on your journey: your own personality and the sowing and reaping principle.

The tagline of Leaders' Map is "helping doers think and thinkers do™". The better you connect thought and deed, the more effective you will become. The more you apply the *Ut Severis Seges* principle to your personality, the more you will progress towards the destination of your choice.

CHAPTER 3

YOUR ROLES

"The task of a leader is to get his people from where they are to where they have not been."
Henry Kissinger

"Do not worry about holding high position; worry rather about playing your proper role."
Confucius

Leaders' Map

If you want something to be done - find a busy person.

If you are a busy (and effective) person then you will be given more jobs to do. If you are taking the lead in one area, then it is likely that you will have leadership roles thrust upon you or, at least, be given the opportunity.

You may be surprised how many significant roles you have in life. Some of them you are born into, others you choose. Some you are paid for in cash, others you are paid with compliments. Some you will be stuck with for life, others you will change frequently. Some you love, others you... don't. Some are exciting, others are dull. Some you compete for, others you are the only one who is willing to do it. Add all your roles together and it makes up a very large part of your life.

There are two sets of jars below. The first provides some examples of roles, the blank set are for you to complete with your own roles.

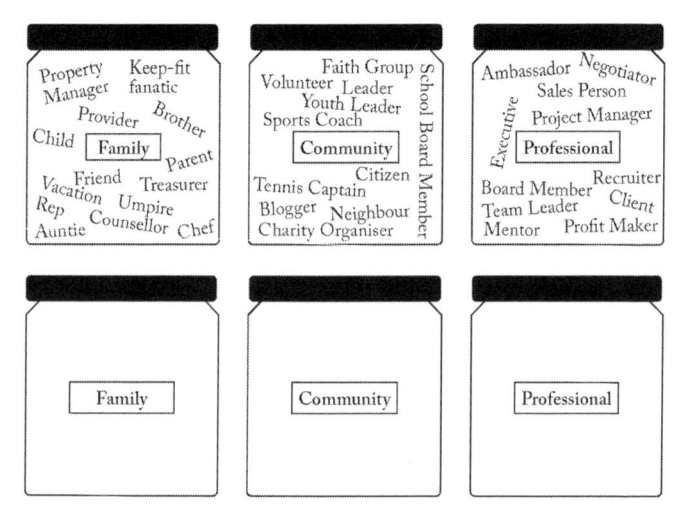

Family jar (example): Property Manager, Keep-fit fanatic, Provider, Brother, Child, Parent, Vacation, Friend, Treasurer, Rep, Umpire, Auntie, Counsellor, Chef

Community jar (example): Faith Group Volunteer, Youth Leader, Sports Coach, School Board Member, Citizen, Tennis Captain, Blogger, Neighbour, Charity Organiser

Professional jar (example): Ambassador, Negotiator, Sales Person, Project Manager, Executive, Board Member, Recruiter, Team Leader, Client, Mentor, Profit Maker

[Blank jars labelled: Family | Community | Professional]

Chapter 3: Your Roles

Now divide your roles into Major and Important roles. By Major I mean a big, broad leadership responsibility like your Day Job. A Major role may encompass a range of Important roles e.g. as Sales Director you may be Team Leader, Speech Maker, Business Generator, Board Member, Mentor, Blogger and Recruiter.

If you have roles that are neither Major nor Important, then why are you doing them? Ditch them!

I stopped counting my Important roles after I counted 47, but currently I have 4 Major leadership roles in my life. Fortunately, this is less than in the past. Focus on your Major roles as you continue through the book.

Getting the balance right

Our challenge is that we have to do it all in 24/7. How can we get the balance right? How should we prioritise?

The common denominator for all of your roles is YOU.

You have these responsibilities principally because of your personality, values and capabilities. There will, however, be some very significant differences between your various roles. Contexts, expectations, dynamics and required styles will vary.

The most obvious challenge is the naturally diverse expectations between work and home. The fact that you were able to close a million dollar deal at 11:00 and you were congratulated by the CEO on the global conference call at 16:45 does not cut it with your five year-old at 19:30 who does not want to go to school tomorrow. This is where "different strokes for different folks" are essential. You are the same person, but the context, expectation, dynamic and style are different.

Switching between roles can be difficult. Recognising that you have switched role is a good starting point. It can sometimes feel a bit like a Shakespearean actor who has four or five roles in the same play. He may have to leave the stage, quickly change costume and return to the stage speaking with a different tone.

Although Shakespeare said "All the world's a stage", you should not be acting. You need to be the authentic you. But occasionally we may consciously have to "remove one costume and put on another" to be effective "in role".

What is my job?

Having coached many top executives I have found that a question they constantly grapple with is "What is my job?".

Understandably, you might ask if they don't know what they are doing, then why are they there? The more senior your position, and particularly if you are in the top job, the less prescribed your job is. It becomes more complex and ambiguous. Why is that?

Circumstances change!

You were hired to "join up the dots", but now somebody has moved the dots around or even stolen some of them!

Chapter 3: Your Roles

You need to be clear not only what roles you have, but also how they can change over time. Let me illustrate it for you.

Do you know how to boil a frog alive?

Well, simply put him in a pan of cold water and he will quite happily let you boil him and very tasty he will be. If, however, you threw the frog into a pan of boiling water he would leap out like an Olympic pole vaulter. It is very easy to be boiled alive and not spot the imperceptible changes happening about you until it's too late.

When you start a new role, however, you have a clean sheet of paper for a short period of time. You can see things with fresh eyes and be more objective.

One of the most fascinating periods in my career was helping to set up three entrepreneurial businesses, which were being spawned out of a traditional engineering business. The CEO, Francesca, was a highly imaginative business woman. She was highly energised by the prospect of creating something new, but, to be honest, she was a bit bored with the legacy business. She felt a bit like the frog in the boiling water having to manage the traditional business, but was excited by the "clean sheets of paper" she could draw on with the new ventures.

Francesca very wisely kept the two types of business apart and both thrived in their own ways at very different speeds. She tried to run them all for a period of time, but was losing focus on the legacy business. Eventually the decision was made to get her to concentrate on the new ventures. It would have been better if she had spotted the changes and made the decision for herself.

Your role may have changed quite substantially since you started it. You have the same title on your business card, but the demands on you are greater and wider. This can be a superb way to expand and stretch your skills and experience. A leader is always looking to develop and to take on the next challenge. But there may be times when you have to say "No" because it is wrong for you and therefore for your organisation.

I have come across numerous situations where people have taken on additional responsibilities for which they are not suited. It was convenient for the organisation, but over time they were boiled alive. They eventually became "collateral damage".

You may be in an entrepreneurial environment. Your situation will then be more creative than created. Your challenges will be both exciting and daunting. You are going into unknown, unexplored territory. A right turn will be a happy event; a wrong turn needs quick remedial action because consequences can be severe. Agility, the ability to adjust, is a key characteristic that you will need to develop.

Remember, ultimately it is your responsibility to ensure that you are in the right job. Don't assume that others always know best. You have to take the lead.

As you go through the rest of the book you will be challenged to think deeply about the various roles that you have to juggle. Be clear in your own mind where your priorities lie.

Also recognise that circumstances can change your environment, either dynamically or incrementally. This can result in a change of expectations. You will then need to be clear in your mind when you answer the question "Well, what is my job now?".

Moving forward

"Okay, so I've thought about my personality and style and my various roles and responsibilities. We know where we are going, so let's get going!" says Dan Doer. "Just wait a moment" retorts Tom Thinker, "Where's the map? We need to plan it."

Who is right and who is wrong? Well, perhaps it's not a question of right or wrong. It is just that they need to work together. As we have already said, each of us has a Dan Doer and Tom Thinker in our own make-up, and they will need to work together – every day!

Let's do some mapping.

Section B

Mapping Concepts

- 1. Purpose
- 2. Non-negotiables
- 3. Your roles
- 4. Mapping your journey

A. Setting the Scene

B. Mapping Concept

Leaders' Map: navigating towards success

- 5. Navigating your way through
- 6. See the Big Picture
- 7. Choose the Right Direction
- 8. Do the Right Things
- 9. Check Progress
- 10. Be Inspired

C. Navigation Principles

- 11. Becoming an All-Weather Leader
- 12. Takeaways
- 13. New steps

D. Applications

CHAPTER 4

MAPPING YOUR JOURNEY

"Map out your future, but do it in pencil."
Jon Bon Jovi

"A map does not just chart, it unlocks and formulates meaning: it bridges between here and there, between disparate ideas that we did not know were previously connected."
Reif Larsen

Leaders' Map

I was brought up when maps were difficult to hold and impossible to fold.

Maps now seem easier, but possibly slightly duller, with GPS and Apple maps limited to the size of a small screen rather than a large dining table.

One New Year, my great friend Neil and I decided to climb Ben Nevis, the highest mountain in Scotland. We had to borrow a map from the rather reluctant manager of the hostel, under the clear guarantee that we would return it in pristine condition.

All was going really well until the light snow turned very heavy and the footprints on the path ahead of us were obliterated. We needed to check the map to orientate ourselves. I said to Neil that we should get out of the howling wind before we opened the dining table-sized map. He was confident in his map-holding abilities. Within seconds the wind had snatched it out of his hands and over the edge it flew.

Amazingly, it got caught on some rocks on a ledge just below us. I then risked life and limb to rescue the crumpled and snowy map. On my return, with worsening weather conditions and low visibility, we decided that to retreat down the mountain was now the best option. I vowed to return and conquer Ben Nevis – which I did one beautiful summer's day.

We dried out the map and carefully pressed it, returning it to its rightful owner. If he only knew!

Chapter 4: Mapping the Journey

Different types of maps

Wikipedia highlights 7 categories:

1. Thematic maps: show features, population, and rainfall
2. Inventory maps: concentrate on a specific feature and show precise location
3. Political maps: boundaries of countries, provinces, and states
4. Mobility maps: help people find their way on land, water, and air
5. Transit maps: routes of buses, trains, subways, public transportation
6. Navigational charts: help ships and planes
7. Meteorological maps: show air currents, weather systems, fronts, temperatures and barometric pressure

Leaders' Map will draw on the Mobility and Navigational themes and may even stretch to the Meteorological.

Leaders' Map is about where you are now and where you want to go. It is about the environment and conditions in which you will have to travel. It is about understanding what will change and what won't change. It is about understanding the opportunities and the risks. Ultimately, it is about navigating in the right direction.

Leaders' Map is unique because you are mapping your future journey as a leader. And, what is more, you can create a unique map for each of your roles. If you were to take a blank sheet of paper and draw a map of the journey for your work role, what would it look like? What is your current position and where are you heading? What are the environmental conditions in which you will travel?

Take 5 or 10 minutes and try it.

Put your map on the table and step back and have a look at it. Every picture tells a story. So what story is it telling?

In circumstances that are very familiar to you, where you have well-trodden paths, things will be quite predictable. You can really anticipate what's coming up. You will need to watch out for the weather conditions, but you will manage. You can build a Road Map and follow the signs. Just keep your eyes on the road and don't run out of gas!

Leaders' Map, however, is devised for something different - where things are less predictable and change is inevitable.

The Leaders' Map storyboard

It is very simple:

To navigate your way to success is like sailing across the ocean… you need to predict the tides… sail through rough seas… around obstacles… use the winds… to get to the future destination you desire… It will rarely be a straight line. You will need to navigate by looking at the big picture and doing the right things.

Chapter 4: Mapping the Journey

We try to get from A to B in a straight line

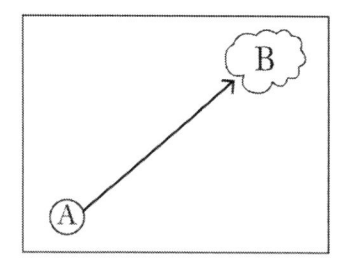

... but life is unpredictable & circumstances change.

Winds blow...waves crash...currents pull... obstacles block & opportunities arise.

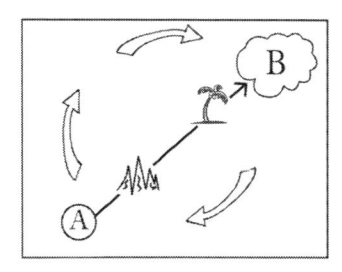

Our journey is more like sailing than driving along a straight road.

We have to navigate towards our aspirations.

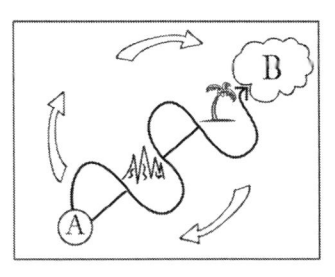

These drawings are one-dimensional, but life is three-dimensional, and with all your five or six senses thrown in. You will feel the wind, taste the salt and take the strain. There will be successes to enjoy and failures to endure. It will be energy-sapping, exhilarating, frustrating and wonderfully challenging.

Your destination and overall line of direction may not change, but your route will need to flex and adapt as you navigate your way through.

CHAPTER 5

NAVIGATING YOUR WAY THROUGH

"Only he who keeps his eye on the far horizon will find the right road."
Dag Hammarskjöld

"The art of life lies in a constant readjustment to our surroundings."
Okakura Kakuzo

I have to admit here that I am not a sailor – give me ball-sports any day.

Having said that, on the few occasions that I have been sailing, it is mightily exhilarating. I was fortunate to have been invited to be "ballast on the boat" at Cowes Week, the world famous sailing regatta on the Isle of Wight, UK, sailing the same waters as many Olympic champions.

The start of the race was amazing as the skipper was trying to get a bunch of novices to be first across the line at the starting hooter. All the boats were jockeying for position in choppy seas, tacking this way and that way, trying to avoid each other and not to go over the line ahead of time. It seemed like chaos – almost akin to driving around the Arc de Triomphe the wrong way – while the skipper shouted his instructions to the crew. All senses were on full alert as we were buffeted by the wind and waves. And we got across the start line first…, but we won't talk about the finishing line!

Tacking and jibbing are the two basic manoeuvres that enable sailors to sail into or away from the wind and zigzag forward.

If you don't make a turn, the wind will blow you way off-course. And it is a long way back. Time will be lost, spirits dampened and confidence eroded.

It is not just the competence to tack, but also knowing when to tack that is important. There are no road signs saying "Tack Left" or "Tack Right" or "Straight On" or "Slow Down". It is a judgement. It is about knowing

Chapter 5: Navigating Your Way Through

where you are heading, what course you want to follow, using the wind to your advantage, being aware of currents, tides, sandbanks or rocks.

Sailing is about using all the assets of the boat to full advantage - the wheel or tiller, the pulleys, the sails - and avoiding being hit by the boom! It's about working in unison with your crew. It's about having good 360° vision and keeping a clear head. Not easy, but it is certainly not boring.

If you translate that into your leadership role you will realise that you have to be super- vigilant and on top of your game.

What should endure?

There are some things that shouldn't be susceptible to change, but should endure. They are things that you can be passionate about, that give you focus and will keep you on the "right lines". Although circumstances may change, these things won't change with the circumstances. They are not up for negotiation. They are the things that propel you forward.

We won't try to be clever, but just use normal business-speak. They are your Vision, Goals and Values.

Your Vision is big, audacious, aspirational and inspiring. You can see it in your mind's eye. You can imagine it. Yes, it may be ringed in fluffy clouds, but it is still very real. You want to get your hands on it, but that won't be for some time. Maybe it will always be just slightly out of your reach, but as sure as heck it won't be for the want of trying. Ultimately, it is why you started the journey.

Your Goals are also big, audacious, aspirational, and inspiring. But they are very tangible and practical. They have a pointy end, and are definitely not fluffy. You can measure them. You can chart your progress to them. They are the trophies and cups – it is party time for the team when you win and moody silence when you fall short.

Your Values are the constant. They help you join up where you are to where you want to be. They were the same yesterday, the same today and will be the same tomorrow. They have a gravitational pull. This is not imagination or a spreadsheet of data; it is DNA stuff. It's what you, hopefully, share with everybody else in the boat.

I have become increasingly aware that although Vision, Goals and Values each have a massive part to play to keep you on the right route, there is one of them that is head and shoulders above the others. It is the one you can't do without. It is the one that is common to all your roles. Values trump Vision and Goals.

Your Values are your "Golden Rules". They are the things that can give you direction and meaning in life. They are core to you. Examples can vary hugely: "Relationships come first"… "I hate waste"… "You can't trust anybody"… "Be totally reliable"... "Cash is king"… "Speak the truth"… "Always deliver my best"… "Don't worry, I'll do it tomorrow".

Chapter 5: Navigating Your Way Through

You may never have worked out what your values are. Or maybe your values might have been ignored or have lost their sheen. It is also possible that you may need to ditch some "intruder" values. Be clear about your values and they can help you to stay on track.

Give some time to clarify your top three Values or Golden Rules.

We will be examining more about Vision, Values and Goals in the coming chapters, but meanwhile we now need to introduce five principles that will help you navigate well.

The five Leaders' Map principles

There is no silver bullet. There is no script or instruction manual that will help you take the lead.

The "technical knowledge" that has enabled you to do a great job is important, as are the management skills that have helped you to advance. The leadership bookshelves have many outstanding volumes that can take you through strategy development to stakeholder-influencing to change implementation. My singular focus is to highlight a navigational framework and some enduring principles that will help you to journey more effectively in whichever role you choose.

I have chosen five principles. Each principle is prefaced by a verb: See, Choose, Do, Check, Be.

Inevitably some will come more naturally to you than others – that is certainly the case with me. Don't just go

Leaders' Map

with the easy pickings. View them as tools or weapons or cards that you can utilise at any time. Just make sure that you pick up the right one for the situation!

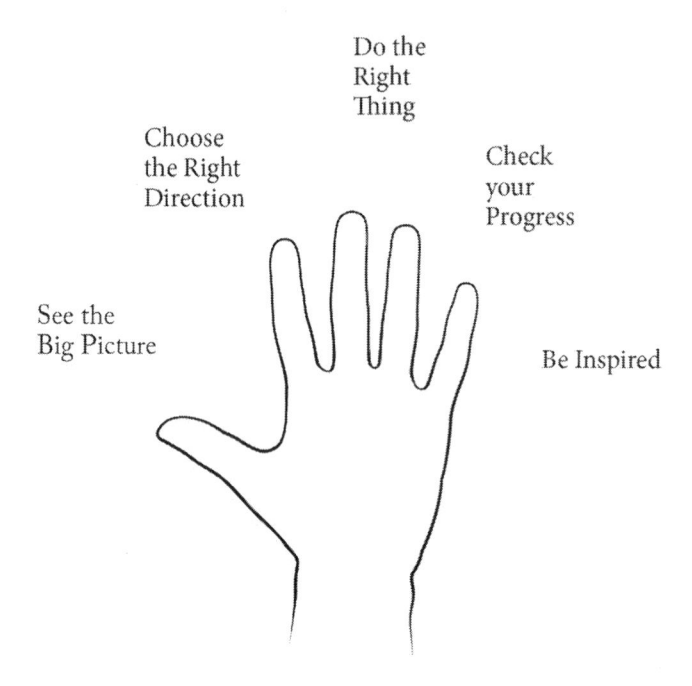

Do the
Right
Thing

Choose
the Right
Direction

Check
your
Progress

See the
Big Picture

Be Inspired

Section C

Navigation Principles

- 1. Purpose
- 2. Non-negotiables
- 3. Your roles
- 4. Mapping your journey

A. Setting the Scene

B. Mapping Concept

Leaders' Map: navigating towards success

- 5. Navigating your way through
- 6. See the Big Picture
- 7. Choose the Right Direction
- 8. Do the Right Things
- 9. Check Progress
- 10. Be Inspired
- 11. Becoming an All-Weather Leader
- 12. Takeaways
- 13. New steps

D. Applications

C. Navigation Principles

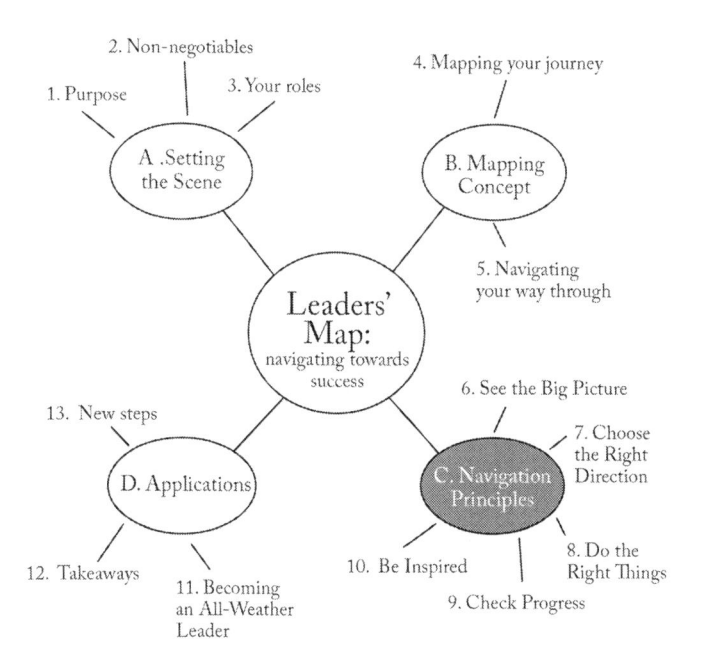

CHAPTER 6

SEE THE BIG PICTURE

"Where there is no vision, the people perish."
Proverbs chapter 29 verse 18

"My interest is in the future because I am going to spend the rest of my life there."
Charles Kettering

You may say that the big picture is "above my pay grade" – it's somebody else's job. For many of us, however, it's because we are too occupied and we can't slow down, just like the hamster on a wheel.

Life can get so crowded that our eyes are pointed to just in front of our toes. That unfortunately provides a very limited perspective. Inevitably, our view will be narrow.

Can I share a "wow" moment?

As a student I did some voluntary work in South India and then did a grand tour of the sub-continent. A highlight was visiting the city of Agra in the north. I got up early in readiness to see the sights and headed off on a cycle rickshaw. When I arrived at my destination I hopped out, paid my rupees and headed off through the early morning crowds. My recollection was of hustle and bustle and everything crowding in as I was looking where I was going, with my head slightly down as I entered through some gates. Then I looked up and suddenly I was confronted with the most amazing vista - the Taj Mahal.

It was breathtaking. Beautifully crafted, symmetrical white marble against the azure sky. I had never been so captivated by a building. The impact of the change from "head down" to "head up" was remarkable.

In my day I was pretty good at football (soccer to our American friends, but football to the rest of the planet!). I was a striker – scoring goals was the name of the game. I had good speed and ball control and knew where the back of the net was. My tendency was to keep my eye

Chapter 6: See the Big Picture

on the ball, which was no bad thing, but it meant that I didn't lift up my head enough to look around and therefore probably missed some opportunities. The very top players play with their "head up".

To *see* the big picture you have to get your head up. This is not easy but if you understand the benefits that may help. You are likely to be a far better player, you will see some great opportunities, score some goals and the rest of the team will be thanking you!

Understanding your marketplace

So what may your big picture look like for you?

If you are in the early stage of your career, or in young adulthood, "the world is your oyster". You have to work out who you want to be and what you want to do. You will have to make big directional choices. It's all unknown, unexplored, exciting, nerve-racking and often defining. Choose wisely.

Fortunately for those of us who are well down the path, we still have the capacity to make changes, to create the future rather than be defined by the past, but it can be tougher.

Okay, so you have chosen your general marketplace. You may be an entrepreneur in social media or retail, you could be Software Sales Vice-President, School Principal, Sports Club Manager, Church Pastor, Head of a Social Enterprise, taking up your first role in Team Leadership or be Family CEO, but you now have to be clear about your <u>specific</u> marketplace. Ask yourself the following questions:

- Who is your customer?
- What does your customer need?
- What do you want to do for your customer?

It is worth writing down your answers to crystallise your thinking.

Peter Drucker, whose writings contributed to the practical foundations of modern business, said "The purpose of business is to create a customer".

Your marketplace could be huge (everybody on LinkedIn) or it may be very niche (three kids, two dogs, a cat, a husband and a grandmother). If you change who you want your customers to be, then you will be changing your marketplace. There is no point setting up your free-range beef stall at the vegan market. You may pick up a few lapsed vegetarians, but you won't be making a profit.

Now you know your marketplace you can have a good look at that big picture. You know that it will be a journey and that you won't be standing still, so you need to see what's going on.

What changes are happening? What is the dynamic? What are the weather conditions? What are the tides and currents? What are the opportunities and risks? You can start to paint your own picture and draw some conclusions.

Chapter 6: See the Big Picture

Let us now take a look at three particular dynamics that will have an impact on your line of direction. We will use the Macro, Meso, Micro concepts again, but slightly differently from Chapter 2.

The Macro view

What big stuff is happening in the world? What are the economic trends? What are you observing in the media? What are politicians majoring on? What are you hearing in your office? What are you seeing with your own eyes in the high street? What would your bank manager say? What have your suppliers told you? What is your best competitor doing differently and why? What do your kids want to do, buy and watch?

For those with MBAs you can factor these points into your strategy plan. I am less interested here in how to put together next year's business plan than about playing with your "head up". It's about game awareness, about seeing what's going on.

The Meso View

This mid-tier is really important because this directly affects you today. It's about the organisation that you are in.

One of the fun aspects of my consulting job is that I get to see lots of different organisations. Each one is an organism – a living, dynamic thing. Someone had an idea and kicked it off, at a specific time, in a specific place for a specific purpose. That has huge influence on the thinking of your organisation – it is the original DNA. Your organisation might be young, it might be old, it could be tired, it may be thriving, it could be overspent, it could be a wild adolescent or you may be just about to launch a brand new one. Each one is unique.

How would you describe your organisation? What do you like about it? What's changing in your organisation? What would you like to change? Where do you fit in? How does it help you to do your job? How does it limit what you can do? Where would you like to fit? And in true JFK fashion, what can you do for your organisation?

Jot down your observations on a piece of paper. Discuss these with a trusted colleague.

The Micro View

Now we are talking about your personal situation – your role. There are two aspects to your role. There is the position you have and also how you actually play. A sports star may have a number 7 on the back of his shirt, but because of his personality he adds something else. He could be the creative genius or the team tactician or Mr Motivator or even the team comedian.

What is your job? What is expected of you? What do you love about it? What do others appreciate about you? When do others get frustrated with you? What is the potential of the role? What do you expect of yourself?

Chapter 6: See the Big Picture

What is your immediate environment like "on your boat"? What would you like to make better? What would you like to change that can be changed?

By taking Macro, Meso and Micro views you have invaluable, real-time perspectives about your journey. With these observations in the front of your mind you can begin to spot and assess both opportunities and risks.

Opportunities & Risks

Francis Bacon said "A wise man will make more opportunities than he finds".

Start to list things that have real potential.

What might help you to progress? For example, you could buy a new player, open a new store, invest in some coaching, develop a partnership, discuss a new product line with a client or move your free-range beef stall closer to the town centre.

If you are taking the lead you need to be at the front of the business, alert to the opportunities that can help your organisation thrive. It is also your responsibility to ensure that it survives, that the boat does not sail too close to shore and get holed by rocks or be out of harbour when the tornado strikes or be taken over by pirates.

So you also have to be aware of the risks. What are they? Some risks will be great opportunities in disguise;

others will be threats to be avoided at all costs. Do you have the right people in place that you can trust? Are you partnering with organisations which have the same values? Who is managing the cash? Are your processes compliant? Have you built up enough reserves for a rainy day?

Seeing the big picture is not about a once a year strategy workshop, however useful that may be. It is not about being in the clouds, it is practical. It is about playing with your "head up", about being alert and aware.

Greater clarity will bring greater confidence to choose the right direction and do the right things.

CHAPTER 7

CHOOSE THE RIGHT DIRECTION

"It isn't where you come from; it's where you are going that counts."
Ella Fitzgerald

"If a man knows not what harbour he seeks, any wind is the right wind."
Lucius Annaeus Seneca

One of my many embarrassing moments was a good number of years ago when I was travelling from London to Paris on business.

I was catching a very early morning train so that I could make my 10:30 client meeting in Paris. With coffee and croissant in hand I boarded the train. My carriage was surprisingly empty. In fact, there was only one other person in the carriage. I checked my ticket for my reserved seat, number B35. I moved down the carriage, still juggling coffee and croissant, and realised that the only other person in the carriage was sitting in B35, my seat. I decided that wasn't a problem and I would just take one of the unreserved seats.

As I put the coffee and croissant down on the table, I thought "No, I'm going to sit in B35". I turned around, went down the carriage and explained to the gentleman that he was actually sitting in my reserved seat.

He politely explained that he was in the right seat and asked me what my seat number was. "B35" I said. He replied that his reserved seat was B35.

I was beginning to think that there had been some ticketing mistake. When he asked to look at my ticket, I duly showed it to him. He pointed across the platform. "You are right, you do have B35, but this train is going to Brussels. That train over the platform is the Paris train!"

I quickly apologised and rushed out of the wrong train and onto the right train. No sooner had I put my coffee and croissant down on the table next to seat B35, than I saw the Brussels train leave.

Chapter 7: Choose the Right Direction

It was a narrow escape. I suffered a small embarrassment, but it could have been much bigger if I had ended up in Brussels instead of Paris. How impressed my clients would have been!

I was starting out from the right place, but I was on the wrong track and about to go in the wrong direction and therefore arrive at the wrong destination.

For whatever reason, we can all end up heading in a direction we hadn't intended or just be plain lost. In this case it was my lack of attention. Once the light dawns we have to act decisively otherwise we suffer the consequences. We have to re-orientate ourselves and get back on the right route.

Making choices

Our chosen destination determines our direction. If you flip it over, our direction determines our destination.

Clarity of direction is essential if you are to gain the confidence and commitment of others. You have to choose it, talk it and walk it.

If we keep it simple it will go something like this:

"This is where we are heading. No, not over there, over here…. This is what we are going to be doing…. Come on, follow me, let's go together."

Please note that you choose it. You don't have to go with the flow. If you don't choose it, you will end up going with the flow.

Apple has chosen to "make a contribution to the world by making tools for the mind that advance humankind". IKEA has chosen to provide "affordable solutions for better living". Nike's choice is "to bring inspiration and innovation to every athlete in the world".

Their choices make them distinctive. They are saying "this is why we exist as an organisation". They probably call it their vision statement. It informs everything they do in their business: who they do business with, who they hire, how they spend their money. It also very importantly informs what they don't do.

If these statements are just words and this doesn't inform how they do business, then they are like a man wanting to go to Paris, but who is sitting on the Brussels train!

Why not ask your team a few simple questions:

- Why are we in business?
- Where are we heading as a team?
- How does that inform what you do each day?
- How do you realise when you are going in the wrong direction?

If you are not happy with the answers, then somebody has not been clear… you!

Your values

Just having the right vision and aspirations is certainly not the whole story.

Chapter 7: Choose the Right Direction

As I was discussing this book with a friend in a café, the man on the next table got up from his seat and turned around. On the back of his tee-shirt it said "The Journey is the Destination". We could have had an interesting discussion about semantics, but I get his point.

How we travel – the actual journey - is critically important.

Have you ever travelled with your kids on holiday, arrived safely and promptly at your holiday destination, but realised that your own behaviour and attitude were well below par? The point of the holiday was to have quality, fun time with the family and your impatience has set everyone back. You've missed the whole point. I have had to apologise for that one in the past.

You have missed the opportunity for conversations about what everyone is looking forward to, for some loud singing to everybody's favourite song and going off the route to have a picnic in the woods and play cops and robbers.

What are your family values? In other words, what is it that binds you together? Just as values can keep an organisation together and going in the right direction so they can do the same for families.

Let's think again about the Leaders' Map.

Yes, clear vision and aspirations will definitely help a lot of people to feel that they are working towards something together. For sure, clear goals will help to keep most people focused and pointing in the right direction. But what is going to stop people wandering way off course and get them back to the line of direction? It's having the same values and upholding them whatever the weather conditions.

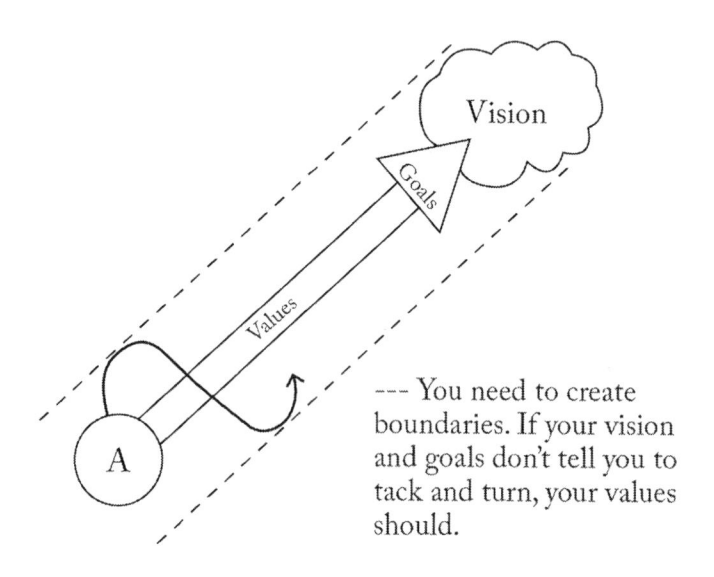

--- You need to create boundaries. If your vision and goals don't tell you to tack and turn, your values should.

If our goals act as the arrow-head, with a pointy end, then our values are the arrow shaft, stretching from where you are to where you want to be.

Remember we called our values, our "Golden Rules". Of course we will have our own individual values, but in a family, a team and an organisation there should be a few common values that are clearly expressed. Although we don't want to be without crystal clear vision or goals, it is our values more than anything else that will give us the directional line.

Chapter 7: Choose the Right Direction

I have witnessed countless occasions when a top performer doesn't uphold the common values. One instance stands out in particular. Pete had been the best salesman for years in a financial services business. He was able to sell big. You could rely on his numbers each year. He was a maverick and a bit of a chameleon. He was brilliant in front of the customer and extremely hard work with colleagues. He had a very siloed mentality – the only thing that mattered was his results. Co-workers felt they could never get the full truth from Pete. Over the years he had a series of CEOs and they all turned a blind eye to him because he helped them achieve their numbers.

When one CEO was just about to move on to a bigger job in the group, the sales director resigned just at the same time. It left the CEO with a problem and he needed a quick fix. Guess what he did? He appointed Pete. It was like a welcome gift to the new rookie CEO. Everybody was aghast.

Within a year all the best people in the sales team had left because Pete was a dreadful manager. Additionally, there were serious issues with the most important client that Pete was responsible for, costing the company millions. At the end of his first year the new CEO was fired.

Who you travel with can be just as important as where you are travelling to. Make sure that you hire and praise people who have the same values; otherwise your boat will be heading in the wrong direction.

In sum, consider your various roles. Ask the same question for each of your roles. It is the same question I had to confront when I got on the wrong train.

Am I heading in the right direction to my chosen destination?

CHAPTER 8

DO THE RIGHT THINGS

"Management is doing things right; leadership is doing the right things."
Peter Drucker

"A little less conversation; a little more action."
Elvis Presley

Frank was "up and coming". He was definitely one to watch.

He was seen as a highly effective operations director in a global IT infrastructure business. When Frank's company suffered major losses he was promoted to a managing director's role.

After 12 months in his new role Frank was struggling. Every stone he turned over seemed to have a scorpion under it. His team was of average quality at best and pulling in different directions at worst. Frank had managing director printed on his business card, but was still acting as if he was the operations director. The bright star was fading a bit.

I asked Frank to look at his diary over the last year just to see what he had been doing and where he had spent his time. Next time we met the weight seemed to have lifted from Frank's shoulders. He explained that he had carefully gone through his calendar for the previous 12 months and segmented his activities. What he saw shocked him.

He had spent well over 80% of his time carrying on doing his previous job. On top of that one of his major contracts had, metaphorically, caught fire and he had become Chief Fire Fighter. He was spending virtually no time thinking about the future or speaking to clients.

Frank was a man of action. Once he realised the right thing to do, he did it. He immediately asked his PA to block out 20% of his time – a day a week - to spend with

Chapter 8: Do the Right Things

customers, existing and new. Nobody was to touch that time.

Not only did Frank re-order his priorities and his time, he wanted his team to go through the same process. He made some key, new appointments and got his team together. In one of the sessions, we divided the team into two and gave them a simple competitive task.

Each team was given a bucket and some materials - a pile of sand, a load of pebbles, three bricks and a quantity of water. It was explained that all the materials could fit into the bucket perfectly. The winner was the team that finished first, but if the materials went above the rim of the bucket the team would be disqualified.

I shouted the order "Start!". One team was clearly highly energised and competitive and launched into action, wasting no time. But within a relatively short time they were retreating, pulling things out of the bucket rather than putting them in. They had realised that the way that they had put things in was not working; the contents would go above the rim and they would be disqualified. It was looking messy as they had to scoop out wet, pebbly sand.

The other team were looking over at their competition rather smugly, as they finally poured the last drops of water into the bucket. They had not acted in haste, as one of the quietest members, who was an engineer, explained that there was only one way to do this. Put the bricks into the bucket first, and then put in the pebbles. The soft sand would then fill all spaces in between and the water would soak into the sand. Simple - if you do it the right way.

Put the big stuff in first!

We then discussed what had happened – yes, put the bricks in first. Frank then gave his view of what had happened over the last 12 months. He had tried to fit the customers in last, but they wouldn't go in. There was no space left.

The light dawned on both teams as to why the last year had been so frustrating for everybody, even though they had worked so hard. They realised that if they did not prioritise their best time to build something for the future, they would be fire-fighters for the rest of their lives.

"Bricks in the bucket" became code for the team whenever they were discussing priorities. The team began to reorder their priorities, responsibilities and time. The start of the transformation had begun, culminating in winning the company's largest ever contract of £750 million within two years. Frank demonstrated real leadership by focusing his time and effort on what was most valuable.

What are your "three bricks"?

We are at our most effective when we simply prioritise what is most valuable and then do it. When we are event-driven and get side-tracked we are at our least effective.

Chapter 8: Do the Right Things

So how can you understand what is most valuable and keep it at the front of your mind?

Let me introduce you to GLEPS™

A New York family had a vase on a wooden stand that was used as a doorstop in their Long Island home. The vase had been in the family for decades. One of the family saw a similar piece in a Sotheby's advertisement and so they decided to put it up for auction. When they realised that the blue and white doorstop was in fact a Ming Vase valued at $600,000 to $900,000 they started to handle it differently!

The rare Ming Dynasty vase was auctioned at Sotheby's sale of Chinese works of art in September 2012 for $1.3m. The owner did not wish to be identified.

A friend of mine heard that a first-edition copy of the first Harry Potter novel had sold for more than £7,000 at auction. The copy of "Harry Potter and the Philosopher's Stone", with an original price of £10.99 was snapped up by a specialist book collector for £7,200 following a bidding war.

My friend excitedly looked through her bookshelves and found her 1997 first edition copy and took it to Sotheby's to be valued. The valuer explained that it needed to be a hard-backed book, but that she might get £3 on eBay for her particular paperback copy. The owner does not wish to be identified!

Once you think something has potential you look at it differently, handle it differently and behave differently. The vase became much cherished. The book received similar love and attention… until it was put back on the bookshelf.

How do you "see" the things that you do each day – your decisions, meetings, conversations, presentations, relationships, emails, interviews, plans, events, phone calls and workshops?

Do you consciously gauge their potential? Do you put a value on them? Which do you undervalue, like the vase? Which ones do you overvalue, like the book?

GLEPS™ is a unique way to assign a specific value to a key decision, an engagement with somebody, an event, a meeting, a task or even your leisure time.

We have identified 5 values or GLEPS - Transformative, Creative, Proactive, Productive or Reactive. We have given each GLEP its own icon.

A **transformative** choice or event will be high impact and could lead to radical change. It is a potential **GAME-CHANGER.**

When you are being **creative** you are generating something new. It could be about strategy or learning or re-energising the team. You aim to "turn on the **LIGHT**".

Proactive tasks are when you take the initiative and anticipate the future. You are being **ENTERPRISING**.

Being **productive** is about tackling important, core, day-to-day responsibilities and getting things done. You want to be **PRODUCING** each day.

You can be driven by events and become **reactive**. A reactive task may add little or no value. Being reactive is not all bad, but you should ask "Should I **STOP** this activity?".

Putting GLEPS into practice

How can GLEPS help you in your work and other roles?

The chart on the following page gives some examples suggesting how you might segment your activities by assigning GLEPS. It is indicative, rather than prescriptive.

As you look at the examples think about the decisions that are on your mind, the responsibilities that you have and the tasks that you need to tackle.

Leaders' Map

GLEPS	Definition	Practical Examples
Transformative	Potential **G**ame-Changer	- Acquire a competitor - Have a baby - Hire a sales director - Start in a new market - Refinance the business
Creative	Turns on the **L**ight	- Develop a new product - Go on a sabbatical - Write an article - Train high potential leaders - Work with your team on the marketing strategy
Proactive	Be **E**nterprising	- Talk to your client about a new idea - Ask someone out on a date - Give your best player a rise before he asks - Offer to help your boss with his biggest problem - Suggest to your competitor that he should sell up

Chapter 8: Do the Right Things

Productive	**P**roducing every day	• Complete your team development plans • Prepare well for your team away day • Mow the grass • Visit each of your customers • Attend your operation manager's retirement party
Reactive	Should I **S**top this activity?	• Meet the sales rep that called unexpectedly • Respond to a customer complaint • Try to solve your production manager's problem for him • Reply to spam • Speak at the sports club dinner you don't want to attend

Please note that "reactive" should not be equated with "bad". Every leader has to react to event-driven circumstances and having the agility to respond appropriately is an important skill. Handling that customer complaint well could even turn out to be "transformative". Things, however, can get into your calendar that you shouldn't be doing. The reactive icon itself highlights the importance of this GLEP – a question mark in a circle - raising the serious question whether you should proceed with this task.

Your mind-set

Your mind-set is your way of thinking. Why not get GLEPS™ into your way of thinking?

Start to think about the decisions you have to make, the relationships you need to initiate and deepen, the ideas you could generate and even the emails you need to write in terms of GLEPS. What is their potential – their value? Are they potentially transformative or just reactive, how creative or proactive will you need to be, or do you just need to be very productive?

This has to be more than a labelling exercise otherwise you will be kidding yourself. For example, you may assign a Creative GLEP to having some special one-to-one time with your ten-year-old daughter. You are going out to see an open-air production in the park and then go out for a burger with her afterwards. It is not the most enthralling production and she is a slow eater, which gives you a great opportunity to reply to three work emails and make two important client calls. That's what you may call successful multi-tasking. Would your daughter agree? Were you being "creative" or just "productive"? We reap what we sow.

By asking yourself, "Is this reactive, productive, proactive, creative or transformative?" you will intuitively be clarifying your choices and decisions, distilling what is most important and crystallising your

Chapter 8: Do the Right Things

priorities. But most of all it can help you to choose your attitude and behaviour. It will enable you to "do the right things" and navigate more effectively.

Many of us will naturally spot the things that clearly have the highest value and those that are a complete waste of time, but there may be 80% in between that is in a grey area. We do it simply because it is just there. There is the danger that much of what we do filters down into the "reactive" box.

If you treat an important business relationship in a reactive way, rather than be proactive, what will be the consequences?

If you think a hiring decision could have a transformative impact on your business results you will approach it very differently than if you think that it is just a normal day-to-day judgement.

If you view the mentoring of a young graduate as a creative opportunity you will prepare for it differently, than if it had just the "productive" label on it.

By consciously putting the right value on an activity you are more likely to think and act in a way that will leverage the potential rather than just get it done.

You are the valuer.

You assign the GLEP. A decision, event or task does not necessarily have a prescribed value in itself. It's your mind-set and behaviour, not the task in itself, which creates the value. For example if I book a meeting with a client it could be creative, proactive or productive. Buying flowers for my wife may be reactive or transformative!

How will you behave differently when something is reactive or proactive? When you think something could be transformative how will you prepare for it? How will you need to adjust your behaviour in a meeting which you judge to be creative rather than productive?

Just by asking yourself these sorts of questions you will start to understand what is going to work best for you.

Find your own methods of making it work for you in different situations.

Practise every day.

Learn by experimenting. You can become your own expert in GLEPPING.

- Make a list of the ten **most important things** that you need to do this next week
- Think through what are the **right GLEPS** for each item and draw the GLEP next to it.
- Choose what you are going to **do today**
- **Prioritise** today's items
- Tackle each item in the **spirit of the GLEP** you have assigned

Get other people thinking and talking about it. Discuss it with your team.

Chapter 8: Do the Right Things

Get GLEPS™ into your way of thinking; let it help you get the right balance of behaviour so that you can be more successful in your various roles, and let it have an impact on what you do day to day.

To support you we have designed an App called Leaders' Map which you can find more about in the Appendix.

Let's reflect on this chapter.

We started with Peter Drucker saying that "leadership is doing the right things" and Elvis singing about "a little more action". So, in sum:

- If you want to understand what your "actual strategy" is, like Frank did, then just look back over your calendar.
- If you want to attribute the right value to what goes into your calendar, specify the right GLEP for that activity – just "GLEP it!"
- If you want to succeed, then just do it!

CHAPTER 9

CHECK PROGRESS

"It is terrible to look over your shoulder when you are trying to lead – and find no one there."
Teddy Roosevelt

"If at first you don't succeed, skydiving is not for you."
Arthur McAuliff

I know of one business where there are two people "checking" for one person "doing". Unsurprisingly, it is not the most entrepreneurial business I have come across!

I also know of a few businesses that were very poor at checking and they are no longer in existence today.

You have to get the balance right otherwise you either become too slow or you hit the rocks.

I was fortunate enough to go to the most amazing day at the London 2012 Olympics. It became known as Super Saturday. I have been to some great sporting events, but nothing matches the excitement of that warm Saturday evening. The standout moment for me was when 80,000 people stood on their feet and roared continuously for the local hero, Mo Farah, all through the whole of the men's 10,000 metres.

He had failed to qualify for the Beijing 5000 metre final, he had won the silver medal in the 2011 World Championships, but now the objective was crystal clear – only the Olympic Gold Medal. The speed and time were secondary, but it was going to be a fast race with all the world's best athletes gathered in a perfect setting. Mo was at the front of the field from the start through to the final lap, but the danger was the element of surprise if somebody broke away from the pack with a quick sprint.

The effort, concentration and tension were immense, but Mo constantly kept looking up at the large screens at either end of the stadium to check what his competitors were doing. He didn't have a rear-view mirror, but he did

Chapter 9: Check Progress

have the screens to make sure he wasn't caught out. Mo was the one who made the sprint for home and to Olympic glory in 27 minutes 30.42 seconds in front of 80,000 ecstatic supporters.

How do you check your progress in various roles?

How do you know that you are on track?

How do you ensure that your boat is not blown off course or, worse, about to be shipwrecked?

Mo Farah used what was available to him. Think through what are the key measures and navigational instruments that you currently use. Normally the tools and instruments we have are good enough, especially for the short term, but the real problems usually lie with you and me. We are the ones who need to get our heads up, use our eyes and ears, ask for feedback and touch things as we manage-by-walking-around.

I guess one industry sector that seems to have a poor recent record at checking progress is banking – which is concerning as they are looking after our money. I worked for some years for a high profile department of a bank, ensuring that they had the right future talent. This department was exceptional in the quality of its advice and service to its corporate customers. They were global leaders in a niche market. The parent bank was seen as solid and safe.

I visited my client several times each week and could pick up the generally calm, but positive vibes of the firm. One particular week, just before our family were going skiing in Austria, we had won an important deal with our client in which we would be supporting them for some years to come. On the way down in the elevator I bumped into the chairman of the bank. He seemed relaxed and at ease.

Three weeks later, after a wonderful time skiing with friends and family, we arrived back at Heathrow Airport in London and I was the one who was relaxed and at ease. I asked my son to buy The Sunday Times just to catch up with the news and sport. The headline said "XYZ Bank on the brink of collapse" – my client! I then did my best John McEnroe impersonation: "You cannot be serious!".

It transpires that even three weeks previously the bank had been unaware of the perilous state it was in. They were sailing along merrily, and had not realised that they had been holed by a very big rock months before and were about to follow the Titanic.

All was happy on the bridge, but nobody had been checking the hull. This clearly affected many, many people and their families, including my own clients who had no connection to the cause of the disaster.

Staying on-course

You may not have encountered such a calamity in your various roles, but we have all, at times, been diverted off-course or just plainly lost the route. It is part and parcel of the human condition.

Chapter 9: Check Progress

It could be as a result of letting things drift, taking a wrong turn, putting off a critical decision, taking a relationship for granted, getting distracted by something that is nice, but not relevant, or just plain laziness and negligence.

The blindingly obvious thing to do is - just get back on track!

Nine times out of ten that is the simple answer. Just do it. But what happens when you seem to have lost the plot… when you seem to be going round in circles… when direction has been completely lost?

Once we realise that we have wandered off-track (or it has been pointed out to us!) that's the time to do something. Don't delay.

But what next?

Well, there are three questions that may help you diagnose what the root cause is. They are questions that you should consider yourself, but you can also discuss with someone you can confide in.

Here are the three questions:

1. Am I still following what I really believe in?

    In a work setting we would call this "our vision". In a personal setting, we may say "aspirations". Whatever role you are thinking about, you need to ask "Why am I doing this?" or, to put it another way, "What's my *raison d'être*?".

2. What was my line of direction?

   What were you aiming for? What was the next goal you were shooting for? Have you hit your last three journey targets?

3. Am I staying true to my "Golden Rules"?

   Remember what we mean by "Golden Rules"? It is your principles, your personal integrity, your values.

Tackling these questions will help you to diagnose where things have gone off-track. If you are not getting 100% when answering these questions then be ruthless with yourself to take the necessary action to readjust.

Being a leader, however, is not just about seeing, choosing, doing and checking. It is also about being.

CHAPTER 10

BE INSPIRED

"If your actions inspire others to dream more, learn more, do and become more, you are a leader."
John Quincy Adams

"To lead people, walk beside them ... As for the best leaders, the people do not notice their existence. The next best, the people honor and praise. The next, the people fear; and the next, the people hate ... When the best leader's work is done the people say, 'We did it ourselves!'"
Lao-tsu

Leaders' Map

"To inspire" according to the Oxford English Dictionary, means to fill (someone) with the urge or ability to do or feel something. It comes from the Latin "inspirare", literally meaning to breathe or blow into. It had religious origins of "breathing in the Spirit".

When we have been inspired we will feel galvanised and stirred.

I play tennis every Sunday morning at 07:00 with my tennis buddy, Julian, on some free public courts. For years we have always known that we will be first onto the courts, except occasionally during the Wimbledon Fortnight, the world's premier tennis tournament.

All of a sudden people become very enthusiastic about tennis and scramble around to dust off the cobwebs from their tennis racquets. There are queues to get onto the tennis courts. After two weeks, when Wimbledon stops dominating the media, the inspiration seems to go and racquets go back into the garage or loft.

I can be just as fickle as the next person with money occasionally being wasted on unread books or exercise equipment waiting in the garage to be used.

Unless the "breathe-in" continues you have not been really inspired, just tickled.

What inspires you to continue? Or who inspires you?

Many of us will have had a teacher when we were at school that inspired us. They may not have necessarily been the best educator, but they engaged with you as a young person and showed you possibilities and

Chapter 10: Be Inspired

opportunities that perhaps you hadn't seen before.

One particular youth leader had such a positive and profound influence on me when I was a teenager. He was a local doctor who gave up his spare time to run all sorts of events and activities. He had a significant impact on many people's lives beyond his work in his surgery. Through example, giving of time and quiet advice he helped me "tack" through those important, formative years. He was probably unaware of it. A few years ago I wondered: had I really thanked him? So I wrote to John, who is now senior in years, to express my gratitude for what he had done for me. For those who are working with young people, never underestimate your potential to influence for good.

Caught, not taught

Inspiration, like influenza, is caught not taught. It may be caught from what somebody says or does. It may be an idea, a deed, a conversation, a view or it may even be something written. It may be caught in a second or over many years.

If we refer back to GLEPS, it is the "creative" icon that we should be thinking about here; the light bulb. It turns on the light – it opens up the possibility for some blue-sky thinking, something fresh and new. How much time and effort should you be giving to this GLEP at your work, or indeed at home?

Stephen Covey used the phrase "sharpening the saw". He used it to refer to enhancing leadership skills and competences, but our motivations and attitudes are really the things that give us the "edge". A blunt instrument is not fit for purpose.

What are the areas that have become blunted for you as a leader? How is this impacting on your performance? How can it be renewed? What would be the benefit to your team?

We could create a very long list of techniques and tools that are available to you, like a personal trainer showing you how each piece of equipment works in the gym. Inevitably it will be a blend of different techniques that will suit each person. You will work out what is best for you.

There is, however, a technique that can work for us all and give us clarity – to see our situation from another perspective.

Distance is a marvellous way to give us perspective. If I could whisk you off to the Caribbean for two weeks you would certainly see another perspective! Apart from the obvious delights, this would help you see the "wood for the trees". Slowly the unimportant things fall away and the "vital few" things become much clearer.

Generally what is happening is that you begin to see again the "Why?" rather than the "What?" and the "How?". This simple process can re-invigorate and inspire. Clearly the law of diminishing returns states that this doesn't work if you spend more than two weeks in Barbados!

Chapter 10: Be Inspired

Our natural human tendency is that we too easily pick up the "Why? What? How?" stick from the wrong end. We tend to focus on the "How?" or the "What?".

When we understand the "Why?" our motivation no longer remains a problem. When people in your team are clear about the "Why?", they become more confident and begin to work things out for themselves.

Creating the right environment

Don't under-estimate the need for you to be inspired. If you are not inspired who is there to inspire the troops?

Let's be clear here, we are not looking for stirring Churchillian speeches or the creativity of a Steve Jobs or the inspirational foresight of a Pierre de Coubertin. It is about leading by example. The leader sets the tone, creates the environment, and lives the values.

Albert Schweitzer said "Example is not the main thing in influencing others. It is the only thing".

Never underestimate the value of being an example and role model. Not only does it influence, it inspires. It can have a viral impact.

I think of Christina who was President of a pharmaceutical business unit. Her core skills were the ability to spot talent - particularly young talent - and then nurture it. In many ways, her team were more brilliant than her.

Leaders' Map

When we arranged a capability audit of her management team, it quickly became apparent that Christina had gathered together some naturally gifted individuals. They were raw in commercial experience and needed a few edges knocking off them and a bit of fine-tuning. Although Christina would not be the one who came up with the most original ideas or the best strategies, she had garnered huge respect and loyalty from the team. Christina exemplified Dr Ken Blanchard's idea when he wrote, "Help people reach their full potential. Catch them doing something right". These young executives were privileged to be mentored in such a positive way.

Years later, those young executives are now spread throughout the industry in key leadership roles. Three of them have travelled further than Christina and are CEOs of large businesses in different sectors. The common bonds and friendship continue to this day.

There is a traditional view that to inspire and influence, leaders must be charismatic, larger-than-life figures. Jim Collins argues, in his book "Good to Great", that the key ingredient that allows a good company to become great is having a Level 5 leader. A Level 5 leader is an executive who blends genuine personal humility with an intense professional will, who doesn't seek success for his own glory, but so that the team and organisation can thrive. Christina exhibited those qualities.

Peter Drucker said "Leadership is not magnetic personality - that can just as well be a glib tongue. It is not 'making friends and influencing people,' that is flattery. Leadership is lifting a person's vision to higher

Chapter 10: Be Inspired

sights, the raising of a person's performance to a higher standard, the building of a personality beyond its normal limitations".

Great leaders create a positive environment where people can thrive and blossom.

The reason this section is entitled "Be Inspired", rather than "Be Inspiring", is because inspiration naturally flows one way.

If you are inspired, then maybe your people will be.

Section D

Applications

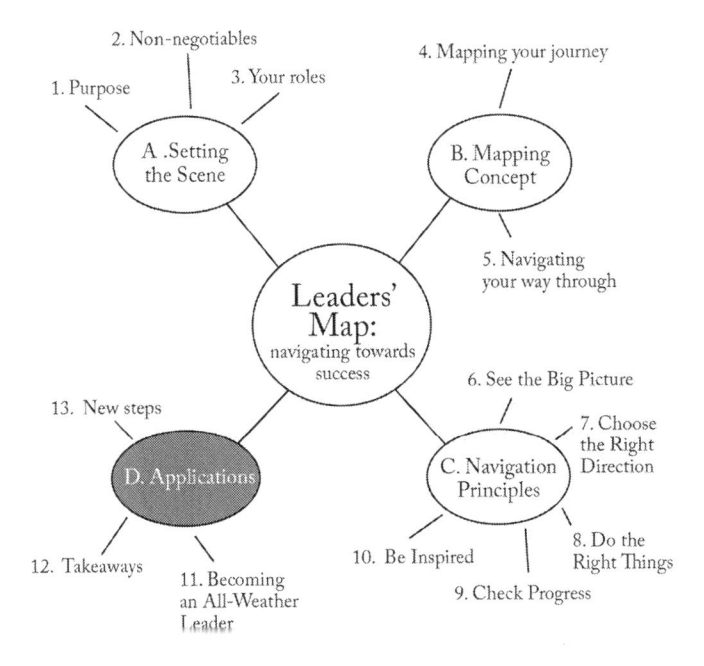

- 1. Purpose
- 2. Non-negotiables
- 3. Your roles

A. Setting the Scene

- 4. Mapping your journey
- 5. Navigating your way through

B. Mapping Concept

Leaders' Map: navigating towards success

- 6. See the Big Picture
- 7. Choose the Right Direction
- 8. Do the Right Things
- 9. Check Progress
- 10. Be Inspired

C. Navigation Principles

- 11. Becoming an All-Weather Leader
- 12. Takeaways
- 13. New steps

D. Applications

CHAPTER 11

BECOMING AN ALL-WEATHER LEADER

"Success is not final, failure is not fatal: it is the courage to continue that counts."
Winston Churchill

"We cannot lead anyone else further than we have been ourselves."
John Maxwell

An "All-Weather Leader" needs exposure to all weathers – and not just the sunshine!

I would define an All-Weather Leader as someone who can survive and thrive through the full range of weather-cycles… and take people with them.

Having interviewed thousands of people, I am always both fascinated and inspired by individuals who have survived and triumphed through adversity. It is a great privilege to hear people tell their story, in a matter-of-fact way, of how they have handled and navigated through extraordinarily difficult circumstances. The quality that is most admirable is their attitude of positive resilience. By that I don't mean a naïve, unrealistic gung-ho "everything's okay" approach, but a view that "I am going to make the best of this in spite of the circumstances".

It means accepting the brutal realities and then making the best response. It means making the right navigational response – the right zigzag.

The explorer

In 1914 Ernest Shackleton and his 27-strong team set off in their ship, HMS Endurance, towards the South Pole. Their goal was to be the first to walk across the inhospitable continent of Antarctica, from shore to shore.

His expedition faced extraordinary weather conditions and setbacks. Their ship was trapped by the pack ice, immobilised and eventually crushed by it.

Chapter 11: Becoming an All-Weather Leader

Their mission had failed. Now it was a matter of survival.

In his diary he said, "A man must shape himself to a new mark directly the old one goes to ground. I pray to God, I can manage the whole party to civilisation."

In extremis, Shackleton had to throw overboard his vision and his goals - but never his values – to care for his men. Now he had to navigate his way through to "a new mark".

Survival was the initial objective. For almost a year their diet was seal, penguin and whale meat. They kept warm using seal blubber oil for fires and kept their spirits up by playing football on the ice shelf.

Clearly this wasn't sustainable. Rescue became the next objective. They were stranded on Elephant Island and their nearest neighbours were 800 miles north at a remote whaling station on South Georgia Island. He decided that he and five of his men would row a small lifeboat the 800 miles to South Georgia.

With little food and water, and no medical supplies, Shackleton and his men braved the ice-packed seas. The journey from Elephant Island to South Georgia Island is considered one of the greatest navigational feats in history.

After weeks, they reached South Georgia. They were forced by thirst, a broken rudder and a leaking boat to land on the uninhabited south side of the island. Realizing that the boat could take them no further, they crossed a previously unconquered glacial mountain range to reach the whaling station.

Shackleton immediately set about to complete his new mission - to rescue the rest of his men.

On 30 August 1916 the Chilean naval tug Yelcho and the British whaler SS Southern Sky reached Elephant Island to rescue the 22 men, who had been stranded for four and a half months.

Long after the events, films and books have been written about Ernest Shackleton and his leadership qualities. He is an exemplar of being able to navigate to a "new mark", stay true to his values and demonstrate positive resilience.

These qualities of an "All-Weather Leader" can be illustrated in many walks of life and different parts of the globe.

The school girl

In early 2009, an 11 year-old Pakistani girl began to write a blog about her life under Taliban rule, in the Swat Valley in Khyber Pakhtunkhwa province.

The Taliban had, at times, banned girls from attending school. She wrote about a girl's right to education.

Her name is Malala Yousafzai. Even as a young girl she became prominent.

I remember hearing about her for the first time on 9 October 2012. I was watching the TV news and heard that Malala had been shot in the head and neck by Taliban gunmen as she returned home on a school bus.

Chapter 11: Becoming an All-Weather Leader

She remained unconscious and in a critical condition. Days later I remember her being transported by plane to a hospital in Birmingham, UK, for intensive medical treatment. On 12 October, a group of 50 Islamic clerics in Pakistan issued a fatwa against those who tried to kill her, but the Taliban reiterated its intent to kill Malala and her father.

We heard again on the television news of her slow recovery, but were inspired by her remarkable attitude in such adversity.

On 12 July 2013, her sixteenth birthday, Malala spoke at the United Nations in New York. She called for worldwide access to education.

"I raise up my voice – not so that I can shout, but so that those without a voice can be heard."

"I don't want revenge on the Taliban; I want education for sons and daughters of the Taliban."

"Terrorists thought that they would change my aims and stop my ambitions, but nothing changed in my life except this - weakness, fear and hopelessness died; strength, power and courage was born."

Remarkable - an "All-Weather Leader" and only sixteen years old.

The poet

Four years before Ernest Shackleton's voyage to Antarctica, Rudyard Kipling wrote his poem "If".

If you can keep your head when all about you
Are losing theirs and blaming it on you,
If you can trust yourself when all men doubt you,
But make allowance for their doubting too;
If you can wait and not be tired by waiting,
Or being lied about, don't deal in lies,
Or being hated, don't give way to hating,
And yet don't look too good, nor talk too wise:

If you can dream - and not make dreams your master;
If you can think - and not make thoughts your aim;
If you can meet with Triumph and Disaster
And treat those two impostors just the same;
If you can bear to hear the truth you've spoken
Twisted by knaves to make a trap for fools,
Or watch the things you gave your life to, broken,
And stoop and build 'em up with worn-out tools:

If you can make one heap of all your winnings
And risk it on one turn of pitch-and-toss,
And lose, and start again at your beginnings
And never breathe a word about your loss;
If you can force your heart and nerve and sinew
To serve your turn long after they are gone,
And so hold on when there is nothing in you
Except the Will which says to them: 'Hold on!'

If you can talk with crowds and keep your virtue,
Or walk with Kings - nor lose the common touch,

Chapter 11: Becoming an All-Weather Leader

if neither foes nor loving friends can hurt you,
If all men count with you, but none too much;
If you can fill the unforgiving minute
With sixty seconds' worth of distance run,
Yours is the Earth and everything that's in it,
And - which is more - you'll be a Man, my son!

One of my father's favourite words was "Stickability". He had it in abundance, but it is a quality that seems to be in short supply in an increasingly changing world. If you are to succeed you need to stick with doing the right things.

In a 2013 New Forbes Post it highlighted that 40% of CEOs are fired within the first 18 months on the job. Manchester United could have fired Alex Ferguson very early on in his career for poor performance. Twenty six years and 38 trophies later they are very glad they didn't. So what lesson can we learn from Ernest Shackleton, Malala Yousafza, Rudyard Kipling, Harry Greenway and Alex Ferguson?

An All-Weather Leader is able to deal with the weather conditions that come his way and make the right zig and the right zag.

CHAPTER 12

TAKEAWAYS

"Wisdom is harder to DO, than it is to know."
Yula Moses

"It always seems impossible until it's done."
Nelson Mandela

Leaders' Map

The best leaders and mentors create insight.

Insight means seeing the true nature or character of something. It is an intuitive understanding. It means you "see into it", you "get it".

Insight beats an initiative because it lasts, it can be re-used. It is sustainable learning. Insight combined with right application, however, is much more powerful and compelling.

At the end of a coaching session with an individual I have often asked the question, "What will you take away from this session?".

There are several reasons why I do this:

1. Their view is more important than mine in this particular instance
2. If they articulate their thinking then it becomes clearer in their own mind
3. We can discuss and calibrate it further together, if they want to
4. If they have verbalised it they are more likely to remember it and be able to repeat it to their partner when they get home
5. They are more likely to do something about it

Our human propensity can allow us to let trivia take over and overwhelm what is most valuable. We get too easily distracted.

So I often take it one step further and ask them to write

down their "takeaways" and mail me back within 24 hours. This twists the process a few turns further. It enhances the prospect that any insights, ideas or learning will be captured, bottled and labelled.

Getting to the point

French scientist and philosopher, Blaise Pascal said something along the lines, "I would have written a shorter letter if I had more time".

Capturing the most important things in a few words is a hard skill, but worth mastering.

In the following pages you can distil, crystallise and begin to articulate your takeaways in three ways.

1. Complete your own Leaders' Map for the role of your choice. Follow Jon Bon Jovi's advice and do it in pencil. Try to restrict each response to 140 characters.

2. Consider your own takeaways as you reflect on the perspectives and insights that others have taken from Leaders' Map.

3. Write down your own takeaways and apply them to your role.

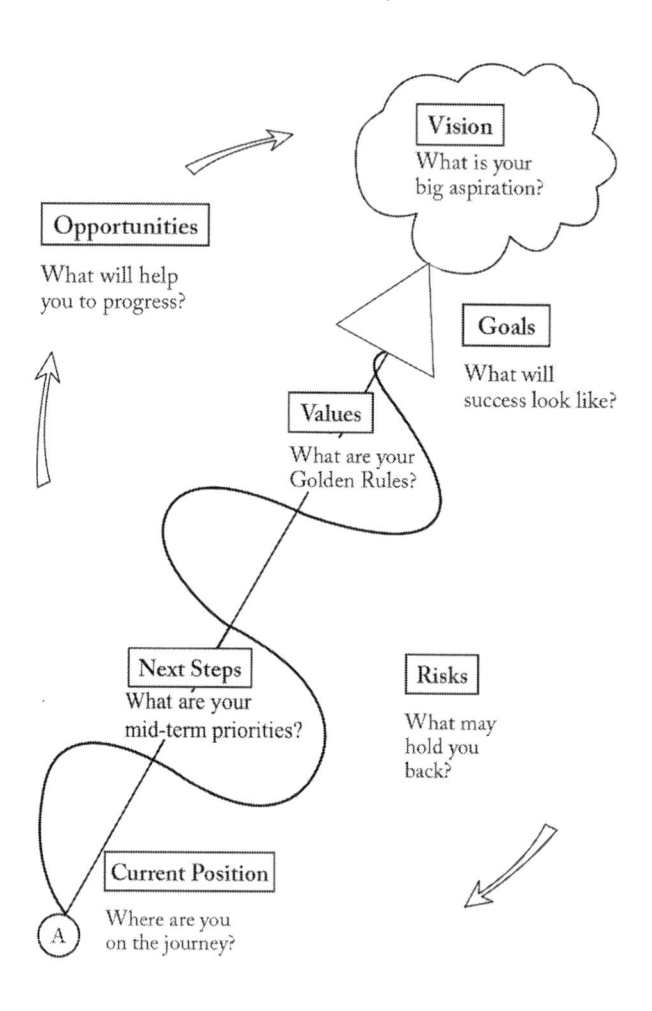

Leaders' Map

Vision
What is your big aspiration?

Opportunities
What will help you to progress?

Goals
What will success look like?

Values
What are your Golden Rules?

Next Steps
What are your mid-term priorities?

Risks
What may hold you back?

Current Position
Where are you on the journey?

A

Chapter 12: Takeaway

Perspectives on Leaders' Map

"As an entrepreneur and sailor the navigation theme of Leaders' Map resonates strongly with me. It is certainly my experience that business doesn't go in a straight line. I will be even more conscious, in the future, of the need to "tack" whilst keeping my eye on my line of direction."
Ed Bussey, serial entrepreneur and CEO of Quill

"A great, but practical concept. As a Frenchman I enjoyed the story of the train journey to Paris. I also have experience that the successful journey is the result of a succession of key decisions – mainly good ones. Often it is only as you look back and check progress that you know these were good decisions."
Yves Couillard, President at Adventissimo and former CEO Hewlett-Packard France

"I really liked the anecdotes as they helped me visualise myself in the situation and how I would have reacted. The most relevant takeaway for me was being able to balance the "head-up" and "head-down", much of which I am already starting to apply in my current business. I will definitely read Leaders' Map again in 12-24 months as it will be just as fresh and relevant to the situations I am immersed in then."
Aneesh Varma, Co-Founder and MD of the mobile innovation company, FabriQate

"An excellent and inspiring read, but most of all very thought-provoking. The stand-out chapter for me is "Do the Right Things", with the story about Frank. My biggest takeaway was the GLEPS concept, which I now want to apply in my own business situation."
Leo Patching, San Francisco-based Chief Commercial Officer for Freetricity

"The map analogy is very insightful and powerful. It is a great reminder to join up the "birds-eye", strategic view and the close, detailed attention needed to get things right day-to-day. The future landscape will be changing all the time on your route and you need both perspectives to be a successful leader."
Stig Bøgh Karlsen, Owner of NoKa Holding and Chairman of several Danish enterprises

My Takeaways

CHAPTER 13

NEW STEPS

"Life can only be understood backwards; but must be lived forward."
Soren Kierkegaard

"The way to get started is to quit talking and begin doing."
Walt Disney

Leaders' Map

Barcelona!

Jackie, my wife, and I visited this wonderfully vibrant city for a short break. One of the big highlights was visiting the brilliant Picasso Museum in the Old Town.

I had a reasonable, but not extensive, knowledge about Picasso. The few hours we spent there really opened my eyes. I hadn't fully appreciated his genius. I felt for the first time I had gained some insight into the artist.

We were wandering back to the hotel through the quiet streets reflecting on what we had seen. There were old, high tenements on either side providing shade from the Spanish sun. There was hardly anybody around apart from a youth loitering on the corner and one or two people in the distance. It was siesta time.

It all happened in a split second.

Unusually I was a step or two ahead of Jackie and all of a sudden I heard a strong, very determined shout of "No!". I turned round and Jackie was in a tug of war with the youth who had hold of her bag.

Once he saw me turn, he sprinted off down the alley, with me in pursuit. It wasn't a normal pursuit ... I was roaring. It was a very loud, primal roar. I chased him down the alley and down the next alley where he had a compadre waiting on a scooter. They got away. But Jackie had kept hold of her bag.

When I walked back, there was a Dutch family with Jackie. They had seen everything and asked her if she was okay. She said she was, but was concerned about

Chapter 13: New Steps

me as I'd run after the youth. The Dutch lady said "I know... I hear him!".

The conversation for the rest of the day was dominated, not by our reflections on Pablo Picasso, but on a potential thief who I was still keen to get my hands on. And what is more my throat was sore for the next 24 hours from all the roaring.

Often we can let our new insights and our good intentions be stolen. They can be stolen by the mundane or a crisis or going down an alley we hadn't anticipated or by just moving on to the next thing.

What is your next thing?

Of course, you can buy the next book or latest gizmo, but nothing new happens until something new actually happens.

Your next step may be an old one. You've been there before. It is the same route, which could be perfectly valid if it takes you in the direction you want.

New directions, however, need new routes and new steps.

We all know how to take steps. We do it without thinking. But if we take a brand new step, we have to be intentional in our thinking because we are stepping out of the ordinary.

Think again about your day job. Think about the day you will move on to your next job. Where do you want to have got to? What do you want to have achieved? What do you want your clients and colleagues to be saying? How do you want to be feeling as you look back on the journey?

Capture those thoughts.

Now retrace the route back to where you are now. Visualise it.

Think about the routes you avoided taking in the wrong direction. Feel the relief that you avoided them.

As you get back to where you are now slow the film right down. Think carefully about the last three steps coming back to where you are.

What was the very last step?

That might just be the new step of your next adventure.

In Sum

This short book was written to help you navigate more successfully in your work and other roles in your life.

I will leave you with one final quote from William Arthur Ward.

"The pessimist complains about the wind; the optimist expects it to change; the realist adjusts the sails."

Whether you are by nature a doer, thinker, pessimist, optimist or realist, I hope that your team will be glad that you read Leaders' Map.

See, Choose, Do, Check, Be… Enjoy the journey!

APPENDIX

Leaders' Map App

To help you apply the principles of Leaders' Map to your work and other roles we have designed an app called Leaders' Map.

If Leaders' Map book was written to enable and empower you, Leaders' Map App has been created to equip you. It is a powerful and practical toolbox that should be "your servant not your master".

The App provides you with five key functions:

1. Roles
   - create plans-on-a-page for up to five roles
   - you can view each plan in "map format"
2. Daily Nav
   - enter your tasks, meetings etc. from all five roles
   - GLEP each item
   - prioritise your top 5 items each day
   - tick each item when you complete it and focus on your next priority
3. Calendar
   - plan ahead and enter tasks for the future
4. My Progress

- set GLEP targets for each role
- check your progress against your GLEP targets and priorities

5. Daily Wisdom
    - receive quotes each day that will challenge, inspire and make you smile
    - build a collection of your favourites for future reference

Use and share the various features and functions with your team and colleagues.

The app, at the time of writing, is available for the iPhone. More information is available on or if you want to gain further insights follow on Twitter @leadersmap.

A final story...

Napoleon was leading his army through the roads of France in the blazing sunshine. He turned to Berthier, his right-hand man, and said "I want my soldiers to march through the avenues of France in the shade."

Berthier replied *"Mon General*, that will mean that we will need to grow trees and that will take 20 years."

Napoleon looked at him and said *"Exactement* - that is why we must start today!"

Start today!

Made in the USA
Charleston, SC
28 October 2014